THE STORMS

RUTH WILLIS

Fulton Books
Meadville, PA

Published by Fulton Books 2024

ISBN 979-8-89221-356-1 (paperback)
ISBN 979-8-89221-357-8 (digital)

Printed in the United States of America

For my beloved husband, Charles M
Willis, we will be celebrating fifty years
of marriage on November 26, 2022. My
marriage has been such a blessing to me.

For our grandchildren, Dennis L Wallace, Stephen
I Wallace, Nadia R. Wallace, and Charles M.
Willis–Jones (affectionately called Chip).

*Tis Love That Makes Us Happy, Tis
Love that Smooths the Way*

—Seventh-Day Adventist Church Hymnal, p. 579

INTRODUCTION

Ellen G. White in 1909 stated, "We see disaster on every hand" (*Testimonies for the Church*, vol 9, p. 11). She continues, "On one occasion, when in New York City, I was in the night season called upon to behold buildings rising story after story toward heaven. These buildings were warranted to be fireproof, and they were erected to glorify their owners and builders. Higher and still higher these buildings, rose, and in them the costliest material was used."

She continues stating, "The scene that next passed before was an alarm of fire. Men looked at the lofty and supposedly fire-proof buildings and said: 'They are perfectly safe.' But these buildings were consumed as if made of pitch. The fire engines could do nothing to prevent the destruction. The firemen were unable to operate the engines."

The day is coming when everything that Jesus has said will come to pass. This world has taken on so many changes in the last sixty years of our lives that there is no way to turn the tide of events that we are currently seeing. The Bible says:

> And ye shall hear of wars and rumors wars, see that ye be not troubled, for all these things must come to pass, but the end is not yet. For nation shall rise against nation and kingdom against kingdom and there shall be famines, and pestilences and earthquakes in divers' places. (Matthew 24:6–7)

The mindset of individuals today is not filled with concern for those around them, unless they have the love of Jesus and Christian values.

With each new year, we have new hopes and dreams, and we are optimistic about what the future holds. Our futures are not totally in our hands as much as we would like them to be. As we see our future passing quickly before us, we marry, build homes, and plan for our families. There is no way for us to determine if we will see each other another day, month, or year. Our assurance rests on the one who knows the future, that is, our God.

When reflecting on all the events that are happening in this present age, we often wish we could turn back the pages of time. The Bible states:

> And as it was in the days of Noe, so shall it also be in the days of the Son of man. They did eat, they drank, they were given in marriage until the day Noe entered the ark and the flood came and destroyed them all. (Luke 17:26–27)

The fact is that we are not in control, and if we were, what would our future look like, considering the way we have handled our lives today?

Looking at the direction this world is going, we need to allow Jesus to have total control of our destiny. Let's put our hope and trust in the God of the universe, who is in control of this world's affairs.

CHAPTER 1

LOOKING BACK AND MOVING FORWARD

One of the most devastating events we can recall happened on September 11, 2001, to the citizens of the United States, without any warning, as a thief in the night. The Bible tells us about how this world is going to end. It is sad to say that this nation has put our Bibles on the shelf. The Bible clearly points out the events that will bring earth's history to a close.

The book of Daniel tells us about the empires that have come and gone. They are Babylon, Media-Persia, Greece, Rome, and the divided kingdoms. Each empire has had its part to play in world history.

There is a chapter in the book of Daniel that describes our day. In Daniel 12:4, God said to Daniel, "Shut up the words, and seal the book, even to the time of the end: many shall run to and for, and knowledge shall be increased." As the years passed, before new technology was introduced, it was already outdated, and technologists developed new and improved technologies. Time is moving so fast that even the smartest person appears to be somewhat confused with the speed of these changes.

There was nothing unusual about September 11, 2001. Our day began like any other in Southfield, Michigan. We started the day with family worship. After breakfast, Charles took our grandchildren to school as usual. We were not aware of any unusual events occurring or, if there were, how we would handle them. We were unprepared for the events that were on the horizon. There was nothing that seemed to be harmful, so we went about doing what we considered normal. Suddenly, our world changed, and we were unprepared as a nation and as individuals for this event. The way we have handled our affairs in the past would not be the way we would need to approach our business after this day in our history. This day would cause us to make serious changes in our travels and living pursuits, taking care of our business affairs and especially in the relationship with our government. Our lives changed drastically on September 11, 2001.

On that day, while taking the grandchildren to school, Charles fell asleep at the red light that had turned green. Charles has a severe problem with sleep apnea. There was a driver behind him also waiting for the light to change. The gentleman got out of his car and tapped on the car window and asked, "Sir, are you, okay?" Charles answered yes and explained that he had sleep apnea. After the light changed, he proceeded to come home. He decided to turn on the morning news. The radio had a lot of static, and after a couple of minutes, the news announcer said that the first World Trade Center building had been hit by a commercial airline traveling from northeastern USA to California. This airline became the first instrument of destruction used to destroy the World Trade Center.

American history has recorded September 11, 2001, as 9/11. The targets were the World Trade Center in Manhattan, New York, the Pentagon, and Shanksville, Pennsylvania.

This attack was orchestrated by Islamic extremists led by Osama Bin Laden. There were nineteen terrorists who hijacked four commercial airlines.

These attacks have been called the deadliest the United States has ever faced.

As the morning proceeded, it became very clear that this was no ordinary event and with no doubt a very serious terrorist attack. When Charles arrived home, we turned on the television and watched the airline hitting the first tower. I was off that day for a doctor's appointment at 11:00 a.m. When we arrived at Dr. Garg's, we were informed my appointment was delayed. As we were waiting, we saw the second tower was struck by a second commercial airline. In my introduction, these buildings were considered fireproof. The towers came down like pitch, and thousands who were employed in the towers were killed in a matter of hours. This was a suicide mission by the terrorists, which we called mass murder.

As the day wore on, as American citizens, our sense of personal safety and security became uncertain. This was not a bad dream; 9/11 was a fact. My question for us is, what happens to our sense of security when events such as these happen? Could it be that we have become so paranoid that everyone we don't know becomes our enemy? Is it that those we once trusted around us are those who we now suspect of being our enemies?

I believe we are our own worst enemies. For example, looking back at the Vietnam War, the fact is, a lot of our young men came back as mental dwarfs, with broken limbs and destroyed dreams of a prosperous life. Most of these former soldiers are to this day very suspicious of everyone. These young men went into the service with bright hopes of coming back home living a normal life. These seventeen- to thirty-year-olds were the bright lights in our communities who came back to a country that rejected them. They fought in war where they saw their friends destroyed on battlefields. We have seen enough destruction in our lifetime to make us wonder how things on this earth will end. The books of Daniel and Revelation have given us the information that we need for the days we are living in. When the doctor gives us a prescription for medication, normally, we take it. God has given us all the information we need to know his will, for our lives—some accept it, and many do not.

As we reflect on the events that have destroyed our loved ones and the destruction that has taken place to this date, there are so many factors we know that have caused us to have become the people we are today. The first is jealousy. The second to me is greed. The third is deceitfulness. The fourth is anger. The fifth is utter hatred.

The men who were participating in the destruction of 9/11 were not concerned about whether they would live or die. These men were on a mission because the mission was more important than their lives. I want to say the end does not justify what they did that fateful day. They died fulfilling a deadly mission.

Now, let's move on to the next plane that was headed for the Pentagon. Charles's nephew's wife, Stacey North-Willis, was a Pentagon lawyer there. Stacey felt impressed to go to another section of the building. Fortunately, that section was not the section of the Pentagon that was hit. President George W. Bush was taken to place of safety. The president immediately set up a program for national security called Homeland Security.

This one event has truly changed the way we go about our daily activities. Many of the citizens suddenly became aware at this point that they needed Jesus in their lives. This was a time when religion became a serious part of our thoughts, however only for a short time. Many of the churches were filled with non-churchgoers, for a very short time. Often, it takes a tragedy to wake people up, and then it seems after the tragic experience is over, people go back to their old lifestyle. We have read what Jesus said when the disciples asked what would be the sign of his Coming and of the end of the world. He explained it in Matthew 24. We are truly living in the last days of this world's history, as people have become careless and ignorant of the warnings and have stopped studying their Bibles and going to church. This is a time when the Bible would give us a deeper understanding of exactly what the future holds. We are now in a different season of events. We have constantly been moving forward and looking back. There have been so many warnings about the time in which we presently live.

On September 11, 2001, we were scheduled for an IRS audit in Pontiac. Charles called the auditor and asked about our appointment. The auditor told him that all appointments were cancelled until further notice. The clock keeps ticking, and we keep going about our lives as though nothing has changed, and we are not prepared for any unexpected events. As years have passed, we have a vague memory of the events of September 11, 2001. In the days of Noah, the flood came, and only eight people survived. The earth was repopulated, and as the population has grown, those after the flood began to forget about it.

Bible prophecy is going to be fulfilled, and we need to be prepared for its fulfillment every day. I ask this question: if tomorrow were the last day we have, how would our stories end, with a period or a question mark? This is something to think about as we look at the events we are now seeing.

CHAPTER 2

A SEASON FOR STORMS

Having lived in the Detroit area for over fifteen years, we were transferred to Grand Rapids, Michigan, in December of 2001. Charles was assigned to the Bethel Seventh-Day Adventist Church in Grand Rapids and the Idlewild Church, in Idlewild, Michigan.

Most parents, no matter how old or young their children are, are always ready to help if they can. Our youngest daughter Sharone and her children were still living in Detroit. Sharone's husband experienced a bad situation and had to serve time. Sharone found herself without a job or transportation in Detroit. I suggested that she and her children move to Grand Rapids and pursue a different future. At this point, she agreed. We then packed their things and moved them in with us until she was able to get her own place. Sharone and I were pursuing an education at Davenport University; she finished her degree in accounting. I was not able to finish my degree in business administration. I still have six classes to finish my degree, which I have no desire to at this age.

Family has always been a priority for us. After several months, our oldest daughter Crystal was living in Pontiac, Michigan, and was preparing to have our youngest grandson on August 8, 2003, at Providence Hospital in Southfield, Michigan. The day he was born, I was told the main power grid had gone out across the eastern portion of the United States. When Charles Milton Willis III was born, he was put in the neo-NEC unit, because of some birth issues. The next day, I decided to walk from Providence Hospital to a nearby Kroger. I stood in a long line waiting to go into the store for over an hour and a half. Then I was finally able to enter the store. I did not expect to be waiting in a long line at Kroger after Charles was born, during a thunderstorm and heavy rain. I was hoping that the lady in front of me, whom I had been talking to, would offer to drop me off at the hospital. Sad to say, that didn't happen; therefore, I proceeded to pick up the items I had come to get. I went in the store and picked up items for myself and some that the nurses had requested. As I came to the cash registrar, I looked outside and saw a huge rainbow. God is always in control, no matter how bad the circumstances appear to be. Storms come and go and in life; we always need to be mentally prepared to make decisions for each situation with the best solutions for that moment. I believe when a fire alarm goes off, we should evaluate the situation and act with the knowledge we have. As we all have learned, procrastination can cost time, energy, friendships, and money.

It was about two months after Chip was born when Crystal moved to Grand Rapids to live with us. Crystal and Chip have been a blessing to us in our old age. Family is so very important.

CHAPTER 3

REFLECTING

There is a new type of storm in our country. It is a disregard for anyone who is not following our rules; therefore, we have put up fences to protect ourselves.

Can we as a nation turn the page when we fail to follow God's law and the laws that govern our country? I have begun to look back at the events that we have become numb to, as if they never happened. Daily most of the deadliest incidents currently, no one appears to care. There are lives that have been or are being taken that are called horrific but then are treated as though they were not real or never happened. As citizens of the greatest nation on earth, we have become intolerant of each other, and we tend to blame others for situations that we have created. We allow our children to have liberties that our parents and grandparents put limits on. It appears that the values that come from home, church, and school are lacking; therefore, love and respect are missing in our communities. Our children have become people without a sense of direction, limitations, or rules. We need to ask ourselves: What do expect from them? Are these regulations missing? At this present time, most children know nothing of any type of religion or morals; therefore, there is chaos in our communities.

The ten commandments in Exodus 20:1–17 were not just for the children of Israel; they are for everyone. I am putting them in surviving the storms because to delete them from our society, we have the violence we are seeing today. In our country, most parents in their forties and fifties have said when they had children, "I am not going to raise my children the way I was raised." To have children without rules is a sin and the worst kind of child development training for any child.

Here are God's ten commandments:

And God spake all the words saying,

"Thou shalt have no other gods before me.

Thou shalt not make unto thee any graven image. Or any likeness of anything that is in heaven above, or that is in the earth beneath, or that is the water under the earth:

Thou shalt not bow down thyself to them, nor serve them: for I the Lord thy God am a jealous God, visiting the iniquity of the fathers upon the children unto the third and fourth generation of them that me.

And shewing mercy unto thousands of them that love me and keep my commandments.

Thou shalt not take the name of the Lord thy God in vain: for the Lord will not hold him guiltless that taketh His name in vain.

Remember the sabbath day, to keep it holy, Six days shalt thou labour, and do all thy work:

But the seventh day is the sabbath of the Lord thy God: in it thou shalt not do any work, thou, nor thy son, nor thy daughter, thy manservant, nor thy maidservant, nor thy cattle, nor thy stranger that is within thy gates:

For in six days the Lord made heaven and earth: the sea, and all that in them is, and rested the seventh day: wherefore the Lord blessed the sabbath day and hallowed it.

Honor thy father and thy mother: that days may be long upon the land which the Lord thy God giveth thee:

Thou shalt not kill.

Thou shalt not commit adultery:

Thou shalt not steal:

Thou shalt not bear false witness against thy neighbor:

Thou shalt not covet thy neighbor's house, thou shalt not covet thy neighbor's wife, nor his manservant, nor maidservant, nor his ox, nor his ass, nor anything that is thy neighbor's."
(Exodus 20:3–17)

Without rules, we have all kinds of trouble that come as a result. Our children have nothing that says, "I cannot do whatever I feel I want to." I wonder how we got to the point we are today. I know why; it is because we don't follow God's laws or the laws that have governed our country, nor do we teach them to our children. The world we live in is broken, and it would be difficult to stop it from going in the direction our country and the world is going in because we are so far gone.

We tend to go through a bad experience while thinking beforehand, saying, "Why is this happening to me (us)?" So many times, we are the cause. I would like to point out that we can often change events in our lives so that those horrible experiences will not be ours. In making changes, we can change our friends, build up our families, sustain stronger marriages, create a stronger social environment, follow the laws, and put our faith and trust in God. The Bible is the best guide to living better. The violence that has come to our communities would not have come if we had treated each other with kindness and respect.

CHAPTER 4

WARNINGS IGNORED

I remember the winters of 1976 and 1977 in the southwestern part of Michigan. One Wednesday night in 1976, as I was preparing to go to work, Charles said, "The sky does not look very good." At that time, I worked at the Memorial Hospital in St. Joe, Michigan, about thirty miles from Andrews University. That night, the snow began to fall. The city received so much snow. As a result, no one could leave their homes, and no one could travel on the street. This lasted three days. Hospital staff members rotated into four-hour shifts.

The best preparation will not always help us in a crisis, as in the case of September 11, the power grid going out in August of 2003, Katrina in August of 2005, or the snowstorms in 1976 and 1977. There are times when the unexpected happens and we are caught totally off guard. These are the times when we need to pray for guidance and direction from God. There is nothing new; history is repeating itself. We need to go back and really study world history and see how the Bible explains the events that are part of our everyday life.

President Bush was not prepared for the terrorists' attack, but he acted immediately, to ensure the safety of himself and the American citizens. Our lives will never be the same as they were before September 11, 2001. Before the attacks, we could go just about anywhere in the world without a passport; everything has changed. Sad to say, our trust in each other has also changed. I sometimes wonder what it will take to wake Americans up. There were ten plagues that God sent to Egypt by Moses in order to get Pharaoh's attention. It took the death of his first-born son before Pharaoh would let the children of Israel go.

The next horrific event was a category 5 Atlantic hurricane called Katrina with winds up to 175 miles per hour in late August of 2005. Katrina resulted in 1392 deaths. The cost of this hurricane was $97.4 to $145.5 billion. Most of the damage was in the city of New Orleans. Surrounding areas did not receive substantial damage. The levees broke, and the water crusted. The levees were not able to prevent the damage that was brought on by the hurricane, and the levees broke. The title of this book is called *The Storms*. This was a storm that many citizens of New Orleans, Louisiana, could not escape. Those who suffered the most in this hurricane were trapped because they could not escape; they had nowhere to go.

So many times, we receive warnings and ignore them. For example, consider cigarettes, drugs, and alcohol. We are often warned, and the warnings are for our protection. There are government agencies like the Food and Drug Agency, the Agency for Dependent Children, and many other Agencies for the betterment of the communities we live in.

In 2009, we went to Houston, Texas, to visit my brother and three of our grandchildren. We saw the devastation that remained in Port Arthur, Texas, four years after that hurricane. It only takes one storm to wipe a whole community within hours. No one could have predicted the damage that would occur from this hurricane. The citizens in Texas were not prepared for a storm of this magnitude, nor was President George W. Bush. We are not in control of this world or the events that take place; God is!

Looking at the events, we tend to try and find someone to blame, and most of the time, we blame leadership, the president.

This world is racing toward a final crisis, and there is no escape. Everyone will be faced with the last-day judgments. There aren't many people today who believe that our world is coming to an end. God said it, in his Word, the Bible. He delivers his message: this world will be destroyed, when Jesus comes. In the books of Daniel and Revelation, God's Word tells the history of the war that is going occurring in our souls. We must wake up from our slumber. If only we could only see the way this world is headed and make the necessary changes in our lives before it is too late. Could we be among those who believe that this world is going to continue as it has with no consequences for sin? There is a judgment day coming not too far in the future. The problems in today's world are largely problems that man has created. God created a perfect world without sin and evil, according to chapter 1 of Genesis. God gave man the power of choice because he is a loving Father.

CHAPTER 5

FAST FORWARD

As we move forward to 2007 into 2008, President Bush handled the crisis with the Twin Towers, and our lives became somewhat normal. In addition, there was a storm brewing in the financial market. Subprime mortgage lending rates were higher for high-risk borrowers than those in the higher-income brackets. Like the other unexpected events that have come, we were unprepared for any type of unexpected new challenges. Looking at the past and the problems we face, most of the challenges are financial. When one group is suffering financially, it hurts the whole economic well-being of most Americans, unless you are very rich.

In 2007, there were candidates running for the Office of the President, each one stating what they thought would help them gain the right to be the president of the United States. Amid the election campaigns, financial institutions began to fold, starting with the housing market. What kind of storm could possibly arise when everything appeared to be business as usual? The unexpected financial storm began to slowly surface with a mild recession.

President Bush had served his two terms as president and was ready to leave the office. The commitment he made was just about fulfilled, and he could go into retirement. Before a new president was elected to the presidential office, the financial storm arose. President Bush was not prepared to handle this situation before his term was up. The banks began to fall; many of the smaller banks were bought out by larger financial holding companies. As Charles and I would watch as certain stocks would plummet, one of them was the cost of a barrel of oil and wheat prices; we could see the actual way the stock market was failing. As we continued to watch as the auto industries were losing their sales market and the banks were not financing auto loans because of a stagnant market, they were in trouble. All the presidential candidates seemed to know exactly what would help solve the economic crisis. Once again, the citizens of our country became fearful that their lifestyles would change, and they did. President Bush became fearful of this situation and had no solution to this crisis.

At this point, the political parties were only interested in winning the presidential and congressional offices. There needed to be the right person at the right time to put together the right plan. There are so many times that we don't necessarily like the political leader, that is, the best one to solve a particular crisis. Looking at our history, we tend to choose leaders that we like because of a particular party, not because they are qualified for the position, but we choose them because they say what we want to hear. In 2008, the battle for the presidency had begun, and there were three outstanding politicians: Senator John McCain of the Republican party; Hillary Clinton of the Democratic party, who was a woman; and Barack Obama of the Democratic party, who was a black man. During this crisis, Barack Obama appeared to be a candidate that could possibly solve the financial crisis; therefore, he was the candidate of choice because he was the most qualified.

We tend to choose our friends based on our political views, our religious views, or, sad to say, our racial views. Looking at the way we choose presidents, they are not the ones who are best able to handle a series of bad situations. I would never choose a doctor because they have been to medical school but because they are qualified to do their job and do it well.

Just a reflection: It was the summer of 1961. I was taking band lessons during the summer at Benton Harbor High School. I listened to a conversation of a girl and an older woman. The girl was telling the woman that she wanted to be a secretary. The woman told her to apply for the job, even though she wasn't qualified and make like you know what you are doing. So many times, we choose leaders that way, who don't have a clue, simply because we think they will make good decisions. The truth is that God sets up kings and pulls them down because He is in control of the affairs of this earth. In the book of Daniel, Daniel explained to king Nebuchadnezzar regarding the dream he had of an image in Daniel chapter 2:19-21:

> Daniel answered and said, Blessed
> be the name of God for ever and
> ever: for wisdom and might
> are His. And He changeth the
> times and seasons: He removeth

kings, and setteth up kings: He giveth wisdom unto the wise and knowledge to them that know understanding.

The election season had begun, and the choices came down to Barack Obama, a democrat and a black man, and John McCain, a Republican. The election year was November of 2008; the voters decided to select Barack Obama as the 44th president. The voters believed he was the most qualified to handle the financial crisis the country was facing. Along with Barack Obama becoming president, the congressional house was controlled by the Democratic party. The party that controlled Congress in 2009 put together a plan to stabilize the country's economic crisis.

The transition of power from George Bush to Barack Obama was with much grace and style in 2009. John McCain was willing to work with Barack Obama, even though he had lost the election to him; he was not bitter.

I wonder why it is that if one political party controls the government, the other political party works so hard to destroy that party. So many times, any progress that might be made will be put aside, even if it is for the good of our country. When I look at politics as it is presently, the voters are the ones who suffer from lack of fulfilling the job requirements. Most of the leaders in our government are only working for their own selfish interest and their political organization.

CHAPTER 6

A CHANGE

According to the Bible, God sets up kings and pulls them down. God controls the affairs of man on earth; nothing happens that he is not in control of. The paths that we choose he has given us the power of choice.

In 2008, for the first time in the history of the United States, a black man became president. Barak Obama was aware of the financial problems that existed, before becoming president. President Obama consulted with economic advisors as to the best way to deal with the crisis. The minority leadership worked hard to divert the attention from a solution to causing the country to go belly up, and the economy failed.

President Obama worked hard to bring the country back to economic stability. The situation President Obama faced to some extent was because he was black. I truly wish that our fellow citizens were as loving and kind as they state they are. Congress changed after two years of the Obama administration. The Bible says, "if a kingdom be divided against itself, that kingdom cannot stand. And if a house be divided against itself, that house cannot stand" (Mark 3:24–25). Our nation is divided in our beliefs, politics, principles, religious reasoning, and moral values. The next six years became so difficult for President Obama to lead the country. Congressional leaders of the opposite party made vows that even if a bill was best for the country, they would vote against it because of their loyalty to party. The main reason they took this stand was because it wasn't hurting them and they were not interested in the conditions that existed in the country.

The thoughts that come to my mind are the following: if my child is hungry and is asking for a piece of bread, I'd say, "Well, I won't give it to you because I love you, and it won't hurt you to go hungry." There are reasons we choose to do certain things; we think we might accomplish a certain goal. Leaders choose to follow party lines because they have the power to make laws that favor them and their political, social, and economic positions. There is one thing that is not something our leaders recognize, and that is, God is in control, and they will face him real soon. This world is about to end, and there is nothing that is going to change this fact. Every person has to participate in the closing of these closing events.

While President Obama was in the White House, there was not a lot of friction. As we observed his relationship with his family and those around him, there was a quiet respect with those around him as president.

The toxic effect of our political, moral, spiritual, and racial divide began to surface, and people expressed their likes and dislikes for each other. The Bible states that we are to love one another as Christ has loved us. No matter what I believe, no one can force another person to love and respect another person. When love is the motive behind our actions, we will treat each other with respect.

Several years ago, we had a 2012 Chevrolet Malibu. We began to have problems with the steering column, which was going out. The steering column had gone out, at the time we didn't want to admit that it had. We would attempt to go someplace, and Charles would try to turn the steering wheel; it wouldn't work. We decided to take it to Penske Chevrolet for repairs; they had it for two days and were able to repair it. The service people never said, "If you drive it, it could cause you to have a bad accident." Caring was not a part of their job.

We have a very special friendship with Mark and Patricia May. When we voiced our problem with our car, they became concerned about our safety and suggested that we take our car to their repair shop, and they assisted us as much as they could. There are times when we could help others, and don't. The love they showed us will never be forgotten. When we recognize that there are others in need and we should do our best to help the needy, we are blessed.

CHAPTER 7

TIME MARCHES ON

As the campaigns took on the specific personality of each candidate, to some extent, many of our Christian values were tossed aside. In this era, politics has taken many Christians to a level outside our biblical beliefs and principles. In our country's history, we have become revengeful toward those we do not like. The 2016 election became a time when the country was not striving to find the best qualities in our candidates. The storm became one of divide and conquer. In this situation, Caucasians became the targets and anyone else who was helpless or those of the lower-income brackets.

When we put people who are not in the same station in life as we are and treat them as though they are of lesser value, this causes trouble. In 2019, a virus appeared worldwide. It was called COVID-19. This virus had flu-like symptoms but was more deadly. As the weeks went by, there wasn't a vaccine to stop the effects of COVID-19, and people began dying rapidly as a result. The virus was carried in the air. The procedures and precautions that came as a result and social distancing, quarantining at home, and masking to prevent people from catching it from each other became mandatory. By March of 2019, schools, businesses, and churches were shut down to prevent the spread of the COVID virus. Our hospitals had begun to fill up with those who were in critical condition from the effects of COVID-19. There were not sufficient facilities to accommodate all those who came to be treated, and many were turned away and died at home. As the situation worsened, if someone brought a family member, they could not stay with the member at the hospital. This deadly taint is still in the air and has not been eliminated through vaccinations. As we reflect on upcoming seasons, a new strain of COVID-19 appears; each one is worse than the first.

COVID-19 could very well be a judgment for all our lack of following healthy practices. I sometimes use public restrooms, and people use these facilities and fail to do something as simple as washing their hands because they don't see the necessity. There are other unhealthy practices, like coughing or sneezing without covering your nose or mouth.

President Trump got the virus and almost died from it. Regardless, he continued to work against uniting the country. The World Health Organization started immediately working on a vaccine. The main problem is that these issues don't just happen. They are caused because we think we are smarter than God. The end of time is upon us. We see all the signs of the end and think we can handle the problems that are part of the end of earth's history. COVID-19 is not the only plague that we will be facing according to the Bible. There will be diseases of every kind. When we acknowledge God as our creator, some things in our lives will change because we have changed our relationship with God and the way we do things. Each one of us is important to God.

The poor and the needy were not immediately included in the plan for financial assistance and vaccinations in large cities like New York, Chicago, and Los Angles when the plague hit. Most institutions were locked down, and sanitizing measures were put in place. I was working at a hotel, when COVID-19 hit the United States. The hotel at the time was booked to capacity for the weekend. Within thirty minutes after it was reported that COVID-19 was a deadly virus, all reservations were canceled. After a few weeks, I started feeling tired and sick. I called Charles and told him I was quitting my job at the hotel.

My husband and I locked down at home, to remain healthy. It has been said, "Ounce of prevention is worth a pound of cure." Our churches were shut down for two years, and worship services were on Zoom. There were problems with the lockdown. Parents worked from home because businesses had determined it would be better for workers to work from home than to take a chance of catching COVID-19. The other impact from COVID-19 was the closing of schools. Children had to attend classes on Zoom. If there was ever a situation the whole world faced, it was COVID-19. It took two years before there was semblance of normal. The virus is still present and continues to destroy lives with different variants of itself. People are still dying from this deadly virus.

Scientists have created vaccinations to destroy some of the effects of COVID-19, but it is still a virus that is a part of the health problem around the world. In my observation, we tend to treat it as though it is not currently a serious problem. COVID-19 is not a sinus drainage problem; it has been a health problem for millions. This virus has caused millions of businesses to close, and millions of people have lost their jobs. The other part of this horrible virus is that families have been evicted for a lack of financial resources because of unemployment. If I had not experienced homelessness as a child, I would not be sympathetic to how seriously this situation affected so many.

Homelessness is something I have personally experienced. There were times I wanted to buy extra shoes, clothes, food, or gas for someone's car. Sometimes, I'd say to myself, "If I were financially able, I would provide a homeless shelter or a place for neglected children."

Charles would say to me, "I hope you are not going to give that away," or "I thought you bought that for yourself."

When I think about what Jesus gave up for me to be saved, nothing is more important than doing what I can to benefit others. If we all can do our part, our world would be so much better. This virus could very well help us see ourselves as the people we are.

CHAPTER 8

WE HAVE TODAY

In biblical times, Israel asked for a king because they wanted to be like other nations. As time progressed, political leaders came and went. Some were good, and some were not so good. Religion and politics were never meant to be combined. This is something that would not mix well together. There are many of our legislators who have a real problem with assisting those in need unless it is to their benefit. In today's political world, it is not how honest a politician is but how deceptive they can be. History is repeating itself to the extent that people close their hearts to love, kindness, and mercy. Our world has changed regarding what is good and decent. I grew up in the fifties and sixties, and times were much different then.

In 2020, it was time to go to the polls and to vote for a political leader for the United States. The candidates were Donald Trump as a Republican seeking to continue as president and vice president Joseph Biden under Barak Obama. Donald Trump was still running with the campaign "Make America Great Again." Joseph Biden was the Democratic candidate, and his campaign was "Build Back Better." The country was struggling to unite and was racially divided under the leadership of Donald Trump. I still haven't understood what is included and excluded in "Make America Great Again."

Looking at the aftermath of the COVID-19 virus, it still has dominance. President Trump was not equipped to handle the effects that happened with COVID-19. In the summer of 2020, there was gun violence and racial tension. It was like a fire that was out of control. Sometimes, we feel we are so much better than someone else is to handle problems that we are not qualified for, than those who would have been on the firing line before.

In the days that followed, the presidential campaigns and COVID-19 became major issues for many citizens of the United States. The physical structure of our country has been slowly falling apart for years. It has appeared that no one has created a plan to rebuild our economy and create a safe plan for the citizens. Donald Trump considered himself the best one for the Office of the President because he was the president. Anytime we take on a position, we need to pray that God will give us the wisdom, knowledge, and understanding to be the best that we can be. There is no success in any aspect of our lives without Jesus. God is in control of the affairs of men, whether we accept it or not. When I look back at my life in 1972, I got married when I was twenty-eight. I am now seventy-nine, and the year is 2023. I wonder where the time and seasons (winter, spring, summer, and fall) have gone. Our children are forty-eight and forty-nine. We have four grandchildren and three great-grandchildren. Time has passed quickly; nothing stays the same in this world.

Our world is so lawless; many people believe they do not have to adhere to the laws. Promises are made to be kept. During COVID-19, the fall of 2019, I began writing my very first book, called *Still Kicking*. I wanted to give my children something that they could have for years after I'm dead and sleeping until Jesus comes. It was suggested to me that I get it published. I knew that I could not afford to pay a publisher; therefore, I applied for a position in 2021 with Meijer in Carmel, Indiana, and was accepted. After working for one year, I was able to pay off the publisher.

Looking back at November 2020, the time had come to vote for our political leaders. As I remember, the failure of every great nation is that it has come from within itself. As great as our country is in 2023, there is nothing that makes our time of collapse any different than all the other great kingdoms that have fallen. Babylon, Medio-Persia, Greece, and the Roman empires fell because of their moral degeneration. We now are living at the end of this world, where right is wrong and wrong is right. Our society has become a world of people who are careless and angry. A majority believe they only need to please themselves and could care less who they hurt. If we as adults don't follow rules, what do we expect of those closest to us?

The closing signs are rapid. The winds of strife are at our doorsteps. Donald Trump campaigned to remain president by saying he won the election after Joseph Biden. Joseph Biden clearly won the election. Donald Trump has spent two years denying that he lost the election and has caused a disfunction in our government. When we attempt to place ourselves in a position that is not ours by force, we place others in a dangerous situation. Our country will never be the same as it was before Donald Trump took the presidency.

The day was January 6, and the electors were to verify the electoral count for Joseph Biden's presidency. As Charles and I were watching CNN, suddenly, Wolf Blitzer broke in with "Breaking News." The congressional building was being stormed by an angry mob. The police were not able to stop this crowd. The sad thing is it appears that the former president had incited that crowd. There has come a division in the United States because of the election for those who feel they are socially and financially left out. The insurrection was not an event that just happened; it was planned. In my observation, those who stormed the congressional building were those who felt they needed to force those of influence to accept them. The problem is that they are now considered criminals and still not accepted.

As I was reflecting on the election of 2020, I remembered a few years ago there was an election that I thought should have been different from the election in the 1990s. As the votes were being cast and as the results were reported, I said, "Lord please change the results." I didn't want the person to hold the office of the president because I didn't believe they were qualified.

The Holy Spirit said to me, "If that person didn't become president, then Jesus couldn't come."

I want Jesus to come, it is important to me. I realize everything that is happening is within God's plan. We fear the storms, when they are announced, more than we fear having to give an account to God. I believe that we have seriously run out of time. The storms we face are more intense, and the disasters are more harmful. Our country is not the only country where people are suffering from disease, sorrow, pain, hunger, poverty, and death. These problems are worldwide. The only solution for all the storms in this world is for Jesus to come.

WATCH

As I consider the end of this world's history and how every prophetic word has come true, I remember what Jesus said in Matthew 24: "There would be wars and rumors of wars." I realize that there is nothing that we as humans can change. For our reality, we can look at how fast the years have passed, especially with our children and grandchildren it almost seems unreal. Everything in this life is moving faster than we can comprehend. With each new advance in technology that happened yesterday, today, there are new changes in technology. In our minds, we believe we have all the time in the world. According to Daniel 12:4, "Knowledge has increased rapidly." God has set a date in time in which he will judge this world. We can change our destiny, if we accept Jesus as our Lord and Master and keep God's commandments; the choice is ours. This world is not my home. I'm just passing on my way to live with Jesus. Jesus said, "Search the scriptures. These are they which testify of Me, in them you think you have eternal life."

As we watch this drama of the ages conclude before our very eyes, I wonder how we will respond, but then I know, that to some, it is all going to go away as in a bad dream. Wars are not just a part of life; they are brought on by people who feel that they will kill whoever is in their way. The first war started in heaven, between Christ and Satan. Satan became jealous of Jesus and created war in heaven and was cast out. We have family members who have fought in wars to protect and defend our country from ene-mies. As we have watched the war scenes over the years, they have been brutal.

Charles was drafted during the Vietnam War as a combat medic, but he acquired encephalitis and wasn't sent to Vietnam. Charles did his tour of duty at Fitz Simmons Hospital in Denver, Colorado, from November 1965 to November 1967. He saw the tragic results of that war on those who fought. Many soldiers were wounded, with feelings of despair and hurt.

Every war supposedly is a war to end all wars. The Bible says, "That nation shall rise against nation and kingdom against kingdom: and there shall be famines, and pestilences and earthquakes in diver places. These are just the beginning of sorrows" (Matthew 24:7–8). My suggestion is, always study the Bible. It will help you understand what is happening and be prepared for the last days' events. These events will continue to occur. As did the Twin Towers in 2001, we as a nation will not be prepared.

CHAPTER 10

OUR COMMUNITIES

We have come to a time when we make commitments and if we don't like them as in the marriage vows, we just leave. A promise meant in the past that you don't just walk away from it no matter what the situation is. I've known of instances where commitments have become until I obtain what I desire. There are times when we feel that it is not important to keep our promise. A good example would be if you purchase a product or products that are defective, you should be able to return it or be compensated. Most places of business have a return policy. The marriage commitment is different. It is a commitment for life.

As we have watched the events over the years, there is no turning back the pages of history. Look at how our morals have declined, just with marriages alone, with homes built on "if I don't want to stay married, well, I can get a divorce." We have literally taken ourselves out of what God had planned for us as humans in his image. The other side of the coin is that "it does not matter if I think that God made a mistake with my gender." In the Creation, God was the creator of two types of people, male and female. It is not up to us to choose which one we decide to be.

CHAPTER 11

A CHALLENGE

We are in the closing days of this world's history. I challenge you to study God's Word as you have never studied it before. For many in our day, the Bible has become obsolete and unnecessary, but it is the only way we will know what the truth is. There are many churches that stand on God's Word, the Bible, but we need to make it our own study from Genesis to Revelation. Let's review the past. In our day, the lessons we learned helped us build a foundation for life. Today, right has become wrong, and wrong is treated as right. The family unit has become something of the past. Marriage is different than what God intended it to be.

As I have stated before, there are wars and rumors of wars. Time is marching on, as in the days of Noah, he preached 120 years, before the flood came. The people had never seen rain before; they helped build the arch; they mocked Noah. When the flood came, only eight people were saved in the ark. Rain began to fall, and the door of the ark was shut; it was too late to enter the ark.

We are in the same type of situation, regarding unbelief in our world today. Very soon, our opportunity will end to ready ourselves, for the climax of this world's history. In the case of Sodom and Gomorrah, the people of those cities made fun of Lot and considered him out his mind. There were only three people saved when God destroyed those cities. A time of trouble is coming, and God has given us his Word so that we might prepare ourselves before Jesus comes. We all have the warning that we need for the end of time. Let us reflect on the events over the past twelve years and remember their sequence, just in that short period of time.

CHAPTER 12

EVERY DAY IS A BLESSING

As I conclude with *The Storms*, I am amazed that I am finishing this book so quickly. Life on this earth is a serious matter. We have lived through wars, famines, deceases, and storms that have brought with them death and destruction. There are critical areas that have had such impacts and our broken society that include people who are broken mentally and emotionally. Because of our broken commitments, which are made and not kept, we bring children into our lives. As time goes on, our monetary system will eventually become cashless. There are so many reasons this world is coming to an end, and we need to prepare ourselves for it. Can we imagine how things would be if God allowed time to go on another 300 years? Personally, I would not want to be around this world, with all the violence another 300 years, let alone another 60 years with all the destruction of human life in the past and in our present. I am pleading with my readers to spend time learning about Jesus and how to keep all of God's commandments. God has said in the Bible that this world is going to come to an end. I look forward to the Second Coming of Christ as stated in the book of Revelation. What have we contributed to making our world a better place for our families? Let's prepare for Jesus's Coming.

About the Author

I am the wife of Charles M. Willis, a retired Seventh-day Adventist pastor of forty years. I have two daughters, that I enjoyed raising and guiding them as they grew. I have four grandchildren and three great grandchildren, that I love dearly. I taught early child development for almost seventeen years.